THEN & NOW®

HANFORD

OPPOSITE: This image was captured during payday at the Caminol Company on March 1, 1939. Retail sales manager Floyd Bollenbacher receives his pay in cash, known as "Caminol Dollars" in the oil refinery's earlier years. Also of interest in this Powell Studio photograph is the Beacon Security Gasoline ad hanging behind Bollenbacher's smoking pipe. Caminol would later change its name to Beacon. Open for business in 1931, the plant was dismantled in 1990. (Courtesy the Kings County Library.)

THEN & NOW®

HANFORD

Steve R. Rogers

This book is dedicated to my son, Taylor, who not only took a number of the images in this book, but also held the ladder steady for me while I played photographer, too.

ISBN 978-0-7385-9311-1

Library of Congress Control Number: 2011938057

Published by Arcadia Publishing
Charleston, South Carolina

Printed in the United States of America

For all general information, please contact Arcadia Publishing:
Telephone 843-853-2070
Fax 843-853-0044
E-mail sales@arcadiapublishing.com
For customer service and orders:
Toll-Free 1-888-313-2665

Visit us on the Internet at www.arcadiapublishing.com

ON THE FRONT COVER: The Opera House Building is located on the southeast corner of Seventh and Irwin Streets. The building shown in the 1910s photograph was constructed in 1893 at a cost of $65,000. Tom Esrey, a local businessman, owned and operated the Hotel Esrey, as well as a successful liquor distribution business. In 1912, a fourth floor was added, made from wood instead of brick due to weight issues. In 1928, the Kutner-Goldstein Department Store across Seventh Street burned to the ground, but not before the flames had spread to the Opera House, destroying the fourth-floor addition. Today, the structure stands as one of the finest in the city, welcoming visitors to one of the busiest intersections in downtown Hanford. (Then, courtesy Michael J. Semas; now, courtesy Taylor Rogers.)

ON THE BACK COVER: "The large corner building shown here is the First National Bank of Hanford as it appeared in 1911. The structure, which once stood at the northwest corner of Seventh and Irwin Streets, was demolished in the 1950s. Note the signage for the *Hanford Daily Journal*. A trained eye can still spot the now faint letters to this day. This corner is now the home of a Wells Fargo Bank. (Courtesy Michael J. Semas.)

Contents

ACKNOWLEDGMENTS

When I started preparing materials to begin the work on this book, I had plenty of images in my own collection from which to draw. As the book started to take shape, I found myself connecting with friends, old and new, who are not necessarily historical-image collectors but do have photographs of very considerable interest. It was like being a kid in a candy store. I soon found that asking to use these photographs made the project even more enjoyable than I had expected. I have included a courtesy notation next to the images that were either graciously sent my way or ones that I went begging for.

I would like to thank those individuals of Hanford who put in the very long hours behind the scenes to help keep our community anchored to its rich heritage. I wish to give particular mention to the following individuals who have certainly played a part in the writing of this book: Steve Banister for his vision of Hanford's past, present, and future; Michael Semas for his incredible collection of images of which I am highly envious; Randy Shaw for his sense of adventure; Martha Bentley for her knowledge; Dorothea Hamilton for her encouragement; Danny and Libby Humason for all that they do; Dave Jones for his long hours; and Arianne Wing for keeping the ancient lantern burning brightly. Their efforts have not gone unnoticed, and my hat is off to them all. I would also like to thank Gail Lucas and Sherman Lee at the Kings County Library for being so gracious, Sharon Suits for the use of the vantage points from her very historical building, and Sandy Verboon for helping me sort and dig through so many photographs. My acquisitions editor at Arcadia, Amy Perryman, deserves special mention for helping to guide me through the process and making sure the product was a work to be proud of.

Finally, I wish to thank Mom for her loving hand; Dad, who I wish could have seen this book but contributed in ways he never knew; and my son, Taylor, to whom this book is dedicated, for periodically looking in on his old man as my writing deadline drew near.

Introduction

Then & Now: *Hanford* follows on the heels of the highly successful Postcard History Series: *Kings County* by Michael J. Semas (Arcadia Publishing, 2005). Many of the changes that have taken place throughout the decades on the streets and avenues of the county's seat are documented here in photographs and words to help tell a small part of our city's rich heritage. I would invite other members of the community, both the young and the young at heart, to join in the search for local historical information. By doing so, you will be helping chronicle and preserve the many memories that eventually fade with time. Grab a notebook or a camera, and start creating for others to enjoy.

Hanford is a city filled to the brim with enthusiastic, romantic citizens who work hard to maintain the city's small-town charm, even though it is a community of nearly 60,000 people. It certainly did not start out that way. In 1877, the Southern Pacific Railroad laid lines from Goshen to Coalinga through a Chinese sheepherder's camp. The settlement was named for James Madison Hanford, an auditor of the railroad. In a short time, it reached the proportions of a small town; however, devastating fires hindered the community's growth in its early years. In 1887, a fire destroyed much of the central business district. On June 19, 1891, another catastrophic fire once again destroyed the town's business district. The very next day, a town meeting was held to discuss incorporation due to inadequate fire protection. Because Hanford was then in Tulare County, a band of businessmen and civic leaders petitioned the county supervisors for an election to determine if the town should incorporate. The results were 127 for, 47 against. When Kings County was formed in 1893, Hanford became the county seat.

Today, Hanford, along with the state of California and the rest of the nation, finds itself in tough economic times. Local heritage-minded citizens have to work harder than ever to maintain the focus of earlier visionaries and do so with very little financial resources. The China Alley Historic District was recently named as one of America's 11 most endangered historic places by the National Trust for Historic Preservation. However, even with such adversity, the city continues to grow and thrive. Visitors are treated to refurbished buildings, clean streets, manicured lawns, and ice cream second to none. The historic Hanford Fox Theatre continues to provide the very best in entertainment, and young entrepreneurs are bringing fresh approaches to once vacant stores. The city's outlook remains bright because the heavy lifting is getting done. But all of that is in the future and for future discussions. Here, we take a look at Hanford, then and now.

CHAPTER 1

HANFORD'S EARLY YEARS

Hanford saw its beginnings built along the Southern Pacific Railroad. This thoroughfare, known as Front Street at the time of this photograph, is now Sixth Street. Businesses such as Oppenheimer & Company and the Hanford Hotel would help to establish the roots of a community nearing 60,000 today. (Courtesy Dave Jones.)

This early view of life in Hanford on Front Street, today known as Sixth Street, was taken in 1879. Front Street was the original Main Street of Hanford due to its proximity to the Southern Pacific Railroad. The street and tracks run parallel to each other in an east/west fashion. Today, the area continues to undergo changes and revitalization through businesses such as the popular Art Works. Local business owner Steve Banister owns and operates the coffeehouse, which also sells meals and collectibles. A collection of local memorabilia lines the walls, and local musical artists occasionally perform live. (Then, courtesy Dave Jones; now, courtesy the author.)

The vintage image shows another view of what is now known as Sixth Street looking west from Douty Street a few decades into the future. Nearly all of the buildings exist today and are home to significant businesses such as the historical Star Café. The first domed structure towards the rear is the Artesia Hotel. Visible on the left is a park; a public parking lot occupies this area today. (Then, courtesy Steve Banister; now, courtesy the author.)

This view of the north side of Sixth Street between Douty and Harris Streets shows an early horse show in progress during 1890. The first Model T Ford was still some 18 years into the future but would help lead the move from horse-drawn carriages to motorized methods of transportation. These horses reflect the need for strong muscles used for pulling the farm equipment of the time. Several businesses are open here today, including a used furniture store, a liquor store, and a martial arts school. (Both, courtesy the author.)

A Fourth of July parade in 1901 makes its way east on Front Street between Douty and Harris Streets. Many of the buildings pictured here still stand today. Parades continue to be a major outing for Hanford well into the 21st century. (Then, courtesy Michael J. Semas; now, courtesy the author.)

The move from horse-drawn wagons to motorized vehicles did not happen overnight. This 1911 image shows the southwest corner of Seventh Street and Tenth Avenue, home to one of the first service stations in the area. The business was owned and operated by Art Brunell. Today, a popular grill is located on the corner. (Then, courtesy Kings County Library; now, courtesy the author.)

CHAPTER 2

Main Street Hanford

In the winter of 1962, children of all ages woke up to discover that a rare winter storm had moved over the area, dropping several inches of snow throughout the Central Valley. Snowdrifts caused the closing of Lemoore Naval Air Station, located 15 miles to the west of Hanford. Many citizens were caught without snow chains. These daring shoppers and workers braved the storm and helped create this unique Hanford image. (Courtesy Susan Basmajian Akin.)

The earlier image shows the view of the conductor and engineer as the train pulls into the station heading south between Lacey Boulevard and Seventh Street. Today's view remains much the same but with modern improvements dotting the landscape. Thirty-plus freight trains travel through Hanford each day, while Amtrak passenger trains stop 12 times daily for routes heading north and south. (Both, courtesy the author.)

This Hanford train depot was constructed in 1897 by the San Francisco & San Joaquin Valley Railroad. Today, the crossing arms get a workout as Burlington Northern Santa Fe freight trains and Amtrak passenger trains rumble through town on a daily basis. (Both, courtesy the author.)

Located on Seventh Street just east of the Santa Fe train depot, the Laundry Building is pictured in these views. The earlier photograph, taken in 1921, shows employees posing with several delivery trucks. The business was owned and operated by Freeman Richardson. The Santa Fe Hotel can be seen to the left. Today, the Laundry Building houses multiple businesses and office space. (Then, courtesy the author; now, courtesy Taylor J. Rogers.)

These views show the northwest corner of Irwin and Seventh Streets. Both images were taken from the Opera House Building on the opposite corner. The large structure pictured in the earlier image shows the First National Bank of Hanford as it appeared in 1911. The building was demolished in the 1950s. Note the signage for the *Hanford Daily Journal*. A trained eye can still spot the now faint letters to this day. This busy corner is now the home of a Wells Fargo Bank. (Then, courtesy Michael J. Semas; now, courtesy the author.)

Looking west on Seventh Street close to Douty Street, a street scene of old Hanford taken at the turn of the 20th century shows how much the citizenry relied on the combination of horse and carriage to accomplish the daily tasks of the time. On the left is the Aborn Hotel, with the Farmers and Merchants Bank directly behind it. The Aborn does not have to look far for its closest competition; a hotel owned and operated by Kate Jacobs sits directly across Seventh Street and is to the right in this photograph. Behind it is the Cousins and Howland Drug Store. In the future, the Aborn Hotel building would become home to a very popular furniture store that would decorate its display window with Christmas cheer each December. Today, the building has undergone some restoration work and is home to law offices. (Then, courtesy Kings County Library; now, courtesy the author.)

In this Powell Studio image from 1942, the officers of the Hanford Division of the California Highway Patrol can be seen standing proudly with their patrol cars. Identified only by their last names are, from left to right, Walker, Ford, Lindholm, Walton, Carr, Phillips, Rogers, Short, and Martin. Powell's Studio relocated several times in Hanford over the lifetime of the business. This image captures the studio when it was located at 222 West Seventh Street. Clay Culp, uncle to local historian Michael Semas, operated the service station on the left. The building has gone through various business changes and is now home to a downtown paint store. The building to the left is the back of a Bank of the West. (Both, courtesy the author.)

Pictured here is Seventh Street at Irwin Street. A floral plane makes its way west on Seventh Street as it crosses Irwin Street in the early-1910s image. Parades continue to be a yearly tradition in Hanford. The annual homecoming and Christmas parades attract citizens young and old, and are highlights of each passing year. The contemporary image shows the building that was constructed after its predecessor, the Kutner-Goldstein Store, burned to the ground in 1928. Hanford is rich in history; unfortunately, not all of it is good. Structural fires have destroyed numerous commercial buildings throughout the years. (Both, courtesy the author.)

These images are of the north side of Seventh Street looking west between Douty and Irwin Streets. The vintage image shows parade-watchers lining the street as two local citizens use costumes and makeup to drive home an important message of the time. The call for "Good Roads" was a bond issue for better roads linking the commercial centers of towns and cities from county to county. Originally voted on in 1915, it finally passed in 1919. The huge Kutner-Goldstein Department Store burned to the ground in 1928. (Both, courtesy the author.)

These views of the southeast corner of Seventh and Irwin Streets show the Opera House Building, constructed in 1893. The early photograph depicts the building as it appeared around 1911. The Esrey Hotel was owned by Thomas Esrey, a local businessman known as much for his liquor distribution as his hotel hospitality. A fourth floor constructed of wood was added to the building in 1912. In 1928, the Kutner-Goldstein Building across the street burned to the ground, but not before flames leaped across Seventh Street and destroyed the Opera House's wooden fourth floor. Today, a prominent local jewelry store resides in the ground-floor corner location. (Now, courtesy Taylor J. Rogers; then, courtesy Michael J. Semas.)

The Pioneer Day parade makes its way west on Seventh Street at Douty Street in the 1928 photograph. The popular parade was a forerunner to today's Kings County Homecoming parade, which still uses the same route to this day. Parade entries from the nearby community of Armona can be seen leading bicyclers. The structure on the left is the Abbott Building, while the one on the right is the Hotel Hanford. Both images were taken from the Van Sicklin Building. (Then, courtesy the Kings County Library; now, courtesy the author.)

These exterior images from Seventh Street east of Douty Street highlight the many shopping changes that have occurred throughout Hanford's lifetime. The earlier image shows the Cousins Tractor Company and Cousins-Howland Auto Company, originally the Imperial Garage. Later, it was sold to W.E. Davies and became Davies Machinery. While it housed a furniture store, the roof caught fire and destroyed the building in 2001. The owner promptly built a new structure, which remains a popular furniture store to this day. (Then, courtesy the Kings County Library; now, courtesy the author.)

This view of the intersection of Irwin and Seventh Streets shows the aftermath of the huge fire that destroyed the Kutner-Goldstein Department Store in 1928. The fire reached the Opera House Building and ruined its fourth floor. The department store never rebuilt but was replaced with an attractive structure that stands today. The Opera House Building, on the right, is now home to Miller's Jewelry, as well as various other businesses. (Both, courtesy the author.)

These views of the buildings on the northeast corner of Irwin and Seventh Streets shows that business continues to thrive in the heart of downtown Hanford. The building was constructed in 1930 and replaced the Kutner-Goldstein store that was lost to a major fire in 1928. The images face north on Irwin Street. (Then, courtesy Michael J. Semas; now, courtesy the author.)

These views of Seventh Street looking east from Redington Street provide a glimpse of the many changes that have occurred from the early 1940s to the present day. A busy downtown afternoon is shown in the earlier image. The south side of Seventh Street was home to multiple businesses including the Sentinel Journal. Now known as the Hanford Sentinel, the business relocated one block to the east at Sixth and Philips Streets and still publishes a popular local newspaper. Also pictured here are the Purity grocery store and the Hanford Liquor Company. (Both, courtesy the author.)

These two images show the north side of Seventh Street between Redington and Irwin Streets. The Firestone location is now home to a paint store. Sears, Roebuck and Co. would later relocate and expand into a much larger structure one block to the west, then on to a new shopping mall at Twelfth Avenue and Lacey Boulevard. Its older vacated space would become home to the popular Thrifty Drug Store Company. Also shown is Driskell's Appliance Store, later to become the home of an F.W. Woolworth Company store. (Then, courtesy Michael J. Semas; now, courtesy the author.)

Looking east on Seventh Street from Redington Street, these two images depict a bustling afternoon in downtown Hanford. For many years, Seventh Street has been considered Hanford's Main Street, but it has not always been that way. Running parallel to the Southern Pacific Railroad, Front Street, now Sixth Street, was originally the town's major link from Eastside to Westside. (Both, courtesy the author.)

These photographs show Seventh Street looking east in the 1930s and again in 2011. Note the signs hanging above the sidewalks in the older image. A city ordinance against this type of signage would see them removed in the late 1970s. In the foreground on the left is the First National Bank, which was demolished in the late 1950s. Behind the bank and sitting on the northeast corner of Seventh and Irwin Streets is the LaMoine Drug Store, and in the right-hand foreground are the Whilton Hotel, Mode-o-Day Clothing Store, Peter Pan Candy Store, Mirviss Dress Shop, and Peden's Cafe. Ironically, the LaMoine Drug neon sign would later be reworked into a Peden's Cafe sign when the café moved to Lacey Boulevard behind the Fox Theatre. (Both, courtesy the author.)

These two views of the northeast corner of Seventh and Douty Streets show the Abbott Building, then and now. Entrepreneur Kate Jacobs opened the doors to her new hotel in 1891. The building was later renamed the Abbott Building and has been the home to various occupants including Safeway, as shown in the 1935 image below. Today, the building is occupied by numerous businesses including a floral shop and a dance studio. (Then, courtesy the author; now, courtesy Taylor J. Rogers.)

These two views looking west on Seventh Street from Douty Street show that nearly all of the buildings in the earlier 1942 image remain today. From left to right are long-gone businesses Econo Cut Rate Drug, Karl's Shoes, Hill's Bakery, Smart Dress Shop, Western Auto Supply, L.S. Williams, the Brunswick, Tarr's Men's Wear, and Rexall Drug. The large structure on the right is the Van Sicklin Building and is today home to various businesses, ranging from shoes to computer repairs. (Both, courtesy the author.)

The earlier image shows a view of Seventh Street looking west from Harris Street. The Hanford Hotel and the Hanford Furniture Company can be seen on the left, while a Buick dealership occupies the first building on the right. The banner in the modern photograph salutes June as "Dairy Month." (Both, courtesy the author.)

This image shows Peden's Cafe in the 1940s when it was located at 119 West Seventh Street. The Peden family moved the business several times, and it actually burned at one location. The last incarnation was behind the Fox Theatre building off of Lacey Boulevard. The popular café closed for good in the 1990s. Also pictured are Cassidy's Shoes and Rasmussen Jewelers. Today, young entrepreneurs operate a skateboard shop at the Seventh Street former café location. A jewelry store still occupies the building on the left, while a bridal shop is open for business in the structure on the right. (Then, courtesy the Peden family; now, courtesy the author.)

These two interior views show how much time has changed the look and feel of downtown Hanford. The vintage image is of Peden's Cafe in 1940. A trendy skateboard shop is in this location today. (Then, courtesy the Peden family; now, courtesy the author.)

The 300 block of West Seventh Street was the home of Hanford's Sears, Roebuck and Co. store for several decades before it moved to the new Hanford Mall in the early 1990s. The building went through a complete restoration period starting on October 9, 2008, and ending with its dedication, "To our members, our community and our future," on January 22, 2011. It stands as an example of a historical building coupled with a clear vision, both coming together to create a structure the community can be proud of. (Then, courtesy Michael J. Semas; now, courtesy the author.)

This rare 1942 view of the southeast corner of Seventh and Redington Streets affords a view of the Purity Grocery Store. On the far left is the Sentinel Journal Building. The grocery store is long gone, and several banks have occupied the corner over the last five decades. (Both, courtesy the author.)

The handsome couple posing for the camera in this 1925 photograph are Carl and Llda Donaldson of Hanford. Behind the Donaldson couple is the Sunset Garage, when it was located in the 400 block of East Seventh Street. Donaldson was an employee of the company for several years. Today, the structure is no longer a garage. Multiple businesses, including a printing service, call the location home today. (Then, courtesy Jim Weesner; now, courtesy the author.)

CHAPTER 3

AROUND TOWN

Ambassadors of the Hanford Chamber of Commerce take part in opening ceremonies at the rear of the Kings Canyon Savings and Loan Association in the mid-1960s. The business was located on Seventh Street between Irwin and Douty Streets. Downtown Hanford continues to thrive, due in part to the many banks and loan associations that have committed to staying or relocating to the heart of the city. (Courtesy the author.)

This view is looking north on Irwin Street between Sixth and Seventh Streets in the 1940s. On the right are Quality Liquor, Ratcliffe's Apparel, and the Whilton Hotel. On the left is the famous 120 Club, so named because it was located at 120 North Irwin Street. John Scanlon was the owner. Today, the street looks much the same, right down to the overhead wires. (Both, courtesy the author.)

On May 31, 1943, the J.C. Penney store at the southwest corner of Irwin and Eighth Streets burned to the ground. It was rebuilt and is shown in this 1950s photograph looking south on Irwin Street. Other businesses include the Lamme Studio, Hanford Hardware Company, Cregger's Appliances, and Chick's Cafe. Today, the Hanford Hardware building is home to the popular Working Man's Store. (Both, courtesy the author.)

This c. 1915 interior view of the Hanford Hardware Store shows how just about any part imaginable could be found among the many drawers, boxes, bins, and table displays. Today, the building is home to the Working Man's Store, a clothing retailer that was founded at another location in 1937. The current owner started working at the business right out of high school in 1974 and purchased the store in 2001. (Both, courtesy the author.)

This 1920s image looking north on Irwin Street from near Seventh Street shows that the horse-and-carriage combination has been completely replaced by the American automobile. The high-steeple structure is the Methodist church, which was demolished and replaced by the Hanford Fox Theatre. The modern photograph highlights the structures north of Eighth Street, including the Wealth Center Building and the Fox Theatre. (Then, courtesy Michael J. Semas; now, courtesy the author.)

Construction on the Hanford Masonic Temple, shown in the early-1900s image, began in September 1901 and was completed in May 1902 at a cost of $10,997.49. Today, various businesses occupy the first floor. Throughout the years, the structure has been home to enterprises, ranging from a mortuary to a life insurance company. (Both, courtesy the author.)

The Independent Order of Odd Fellows Building, located on Eighth Street between Douty and Harris Streets, was constructed in 1905 at a cost of $12,000. The structure has had many tenants throughout the decades, including the National Guard, the Kings County Chamber of Commerce, the Kings County Welfare and Employment Department, and the local armory. The earlier image shows how the building looked in 1910. Today, it is home to one of the larger antique stores in the tri-county area. (Both, courtesy the author.)

The First Presbyterian Church was constructed in 1913 at the southwest corner of Irwin and Dewey Streets. In 1981, the building was demolished, and a new church structure was built in its place. The church is just north of the Hanford Fox Theatre and west of the Civic Center and Veterans Building. The original bell tower was saved and remained in Hanford for several years, but its location is unknown today. (Both, courtesy the author.)

The earlier view here shows the First Presbyterian Church prior to demolition in the 1980s. The same trees in front of the Veterans Building still provide framing for the view today. (Then, courtesy Randy Shaw; now, courtesy the author.)

This early view looking west on Eighth Street between Douty and Irwin Streets shows the buildings that used to line the block directly across from the old Kings County Courthouse. The large Hanford Garage structure was also home to the Hugo Buckner Garage. The last building in the background is the old J.C. Penney location at the southwest corner of Irwin and Eighth Streets. Nearly all of these buildings have been demolished. A public parking lot now sits directly across from the old courthouse. (Then, courtesy Michael J. Semas; now, courtesy the author.)

The Hugo Buckner Garage, seen in this 1929 image, was located on Eighth Street across from the Kings County Courthouse. Studebaker automobile service was the specialty. Today, a city public parking lot helps ease the lack of parking on Seventh Street, Hanford's main street, one block to the south. (Then, courtesy Garen Goodreau; now, courtesy the author.)

In the late 1970s, fast-food chain McDonald's filmed a television commercial in front of the old post office building on Douty Street near Eighth Street. The structure substituted for a police station in the advertisement. Local citizens would appear in the background but not until after being required to join the Screen Actors Guild. Actual Kings County patrol cars were used in the filming, while main characters were hired actors. The storyline follows the sheriff as he uses the McDonald's drive-thru and orders fries for himself and his deputies. By the time he makes it back to the station, he has eaten all of the fries, and there are none left for the hungry deputies. (Then, courtesy Steve Banister; now, courtesy the author.)

This view looking north on Douty Street from Seventh Street in the 1970s shows the many neon signs that were still in place before a city sign ordinance changed the landscape. Today, many of the locations remain full, but the neon is long gone. A push to bring back the historical signage is underway. The popular Moe's Toy Shop can be seen at the end of the block. (Then, courtesy Steve Banister; now, courtesy the author.)

Located at Douty and Eleventh Streets, the Episcopal Church of the Saviour was built in 1910. An earlier, much smaller church used by the congregation was located at Douty and Third Streets. The smaller church was rolled on logs to its present location, situated just southeast of the larger brick structure and serving as a chapel. (Then, courtesy the Kings County Library; now, courtesy the author.)

The northwest corner of Grangeville Boulevard and Eleventh Avenue was once the home of the Food King shopping complex. After the supermarket closed, the sign was reworked and relocated to the grounds of the Kings Fair, where it stands proudly, welcoming thousands of visitors each year. (Both, courtesy the author.)

This 1940s image provides a glimpse of the southwest corner of Grangeville Boulevard and Eleventh Avenue. The State Market Super Market building was demolished in 1981 and 1982 and was replaced with a location of Modesto-based Save Mart, which opened in 1983. (Then, courtesy Michael J. Semas; now, courtesy the author.)

This 1939 Powell Studio image shows the Caminol Company Ltd. Oil Refinery. The business was located on property south of Third Street and east of Eleventh Avenue. Walter Allen formed the company in 1931, and Caminol used the refinery to process crude oil from nearby Kettleman Hills. Caminol would continue to grow under the new name Beacon Oil Company, one of the larger employers in Hanford. In the 1980s, the business name changed once again, to Ultramar Oil Inc. In 1990, the refinery was dismantled. (Both, courtesy the author.)

At 11:00 a.m. on July 12, 1966, under a hot summer sun, a well-attended ground-breaking ceremony took place for the new Kings Mall Shopping Center, located at the northwest corner of Eleventh Avenue and Lacey Boulevard. A huge J.C. Penney store anchored the mall from the south end. The shopping mall signaled the beginning of outward growth from the heart of the city and was not without controversy due to its impact on existing businesses located in downtown Hanford. The mall was demolished in 1992, and a new Hanford Mall was constructed one mile to the west at the edge of city limits, continuing the tradition of indoor strolling from store to store. Today, a newer strip mall with a popular coffeehouse stands at this location. (Then, courtesy Nancy Parker; now, courtesy the author.)

The J.C. Penney Company offered its own auto center at the Kings Mall. The service center was located on the northwest corner of Eleventh Avenue and Lacey Boulevard. Today, the structure houses both a Sizzler Restaurant and a pizzeria. (Then, courtesy Nancy Parker; now, courtesy the author.)

In 1992, the Kings Mall was demolished, thus ending an indoor-mall shopping experience that had taken place since 1966. Hanford's time without an indoor mall was short-lived, as construction began on the new Hanford Mall at nearly the same time. Today, the Hanford Mall not only serves as one of west Hanford's major shopping hubs, but is also home to yearly parking-lot carnivals and visits by equine stars such as the famous Budweiser Clydesdales. (Then, courtesy Randy Shaw; now, courtesy the author.)

The Happy Steak Restaurant was located on Lacey Boulevard west of Eleventh Avenue. The 1969 image also shows the car wash that was located on Eleventh Avenue next to a Union 76 gas station. Today, a sandwich shop occupies the approximate location of the Happy Steak building. The Lacey Boulevard–Eleventh Avenue intersection continues to be one of the busiest in the city. (Then, courtesy Nancy Parker; now, courtesy the author.)

The Bob Greene car lot is shown in this 1969 photograph. The dealership was located on the northeast corner of Eleventh Avenue and Lacey Boulevard. Statistical information shows that this intersection was the busiest in Hanford for nearly three decades, only recently becoming surpassed by the Twelfth Avenue–Lacey Boulevard intersection one mile to the west. Today, the corner pictured is home to Valley Ford Lincoln. (Then, courtesy Nancy Parker; now, courtesy the author.)

On January 20, 1973, the city of Hanford welcomed its first fast-food restaurant. The McDonald's grand opening included a balloon launch. Pictured here are the restaurant's owners, as well as dignitaries and Ronald himself. Several years ago, the structure underwent a complete restoration as seen below. (Then, courtesy Sharon Alcorn Oliver; now, courtesy the author.)

In the 1970s, the McDonald's Corporation opened Hanford's first fast-food business. Thinking that McDonald's needed competition, Colonel Sander's Kentucky Fried Chicken and Taco Bell were more than happy to oblige. Seen here, 1979 Christmas parade entries head east on Lacey Boulevard, just west of Redington Street. Both businesses have since relocated. Today, a restaurant still operates out of the old Taco Bell location, while a check-cashing business occupies the old KFC. (Then, courtesy Randy Shaw; now, courtesy the author.)

The large brick structure in the vintage image is part of the Lacey Milling Company plant, located at 217 West Fifth Street. J. H. Johnson of Visalia built the flour mill in the late 1880s. To manage the business, Johnson hired Horatio G. Lacey, a Massachusetts-born businessman who had moved to Visalia in 1875. In 1890, Lacey and his two sons bought the mill, and it operates under the ownership of the Lendrum family today. The modern image shows the plant's office building at dusk, complete with glowing neon signage. (Both, courtesy the author.)

The original Artesia Hotel, located on the northeast corner of Irwin and Sixth Streets, was built in 1891. It suffered from a fire that same year and was rebuilt without hesitation by the Hanford Development Company. Guests at the Artesia were once able to use a covered walkway in the back alley that connected to the Opera House Building, which was just to the north. Guests could also take advantage of the natural artesian well in the hotel's lobby, and for which the building is named. The structure remains one of the finest in the city today. (Then, courtesy the Kings County Library; now, courtesy the author.)

The M&G Building, located in the 100 block of north Douty, was built in 1890 in downtown Hanford. The earlier image shows the "doorway to nowhere" after the balcony was removed. The Wenthur family purchased the building in 1996 and completed earthquake retrofitting in 1997. Restoration of the first-floor retail space was finished in 1998. The Wenthurs call the second floor home. The building stands as an example of excellent craftsmanship and is one of downtown's abundant jewels. (Then, courtesy Randy Shaw; now, courtesy the author.)

The Hanford Airport had its official opening and dedication by Mayor G.M. Wilson on November 15, 1930. The day's festivities included a flyover by the Hancock Foundation College of Aeronautics, an "Eat with the Flyers" luncheon at the Civic Auditorium, a 25-mile plane race, an altitude contest, a dead-stick landing contest, an aerial wedding of a young Hanford couple, an airmail pickup, and an evening dance. Today, the airport is still used daily by light aircraft and provides flight schooling as well. The modern image shows young Taylor Rogers preparing for his first flight over Hanford with pilot John Howe. (Then, courtesy Randy Shaw; now, courtesy the author.)

The always-popular Sportman's Club was located outside the city limits near the Tenth Avenue–Highway 43 merger. It later relocated approximately two miles to the south at 1826 North Tenth Avenue, where it was known for its superb steaks and lounge coolness. Years later, the owner's son would become the master chef at the Irwin Street Inn. Today, the former club building is home to a busy spa and salon. (Both, courtesy the author.)

Swinging-1960s fashion is captured in the earlier photograph taken at the Hanford Elks Lodge located at 506 North Douty Street. Pictured, from left to right, are Jim Mehaffey, Carrie Mehaffey, Penny Rogers, and Rollin Rogers. Designated lodge No.1259, it was instituted in 1911. The lodge has a huge flag that makes appearances in parades and other patriotic events around the Central Valley throughout the year. (Both, courtesy the author.)

The Sacred Heart Hospital got its start from six nuns from the Dominican Sisters of Kenosha, Wisconsin, when they established a two-story brick hospital on the northwest corner of Irwin and Cameron Streets. Construction on the 1962 building in the vintage image expanded the hospital to 88 beds. Today, the hospital is part of the Adventist Health Central Valley Network. (Then, courtesy Michael J. Semas; now, courtesy the author.)

In 1973, the old Kings County Hospital closed its doors, but not before staff had an opportunity to say goodbye to the last patient, her family, and newborn child. Built in 1910, the original structure was much smaller—a two-story brick building with a veranda. Since its closing, the building has been home to various agencies, the latest being the Kings Community Action Organization, which left the complex in 2008. Today, the structure remains empty and in deterioration, with the exception of the county's morgue, which operates in the basement. (Both, courtesy the author.)

CHAPTER 4

COMMUNITY PRIDE

Local musicians Ed Porto and the Harmonions were well known for their melodies throughout the states of California, Pennsylvania, and Florida for many years. Here, they shake things loose with a Hawaiian touch in the 1940s. (Courtesy Ed Porto.)

This view of Irwin Street looking north from Eighth Street shows that very little has changed since the early 1940s. The large structure on the left is the Wealth Center Building. Behind it is the Hanford Fox Theatre. The domed building in the background is the First Presbyterian Church, which has since been demolished. Of interest is the huge blade sign that hangs from the Fox tower. The old sign now belongs to a rancher living between Hanford and Visalia. What is left of it is lying flat and being used as a grain trough for cattle. (Then, courtesy Michael J. Semas; now, courtesy the author.)

The ground-breaking ceremony for the Hanford Fox Theatre took place in April 1929. The stock market crash and the start of the Great Depression were just months away. West Coast Theaters, a William Fox company, opened the theater on Christmas Eve 1929, and it has been operating nearly every year since. In 1980, the Humason family purchased the structure and began an extensive restoration. In 1989, a Wurlitzer theater organ was added and can still be heard accompanying silent movies that are occasionally shown. Live entertainment has been the main focus since the doors reopened for business under the Humasons' ownership. Country legends such as Johnny Cash, Willie Nelson, George Strait, and Merle Haggard have performed live at the Fox. (Then, courtesy Randy Shaw; now, courtesy the author.)

A 1948 view of the Fox marquee shows the current movies. *Mr. Blanding's Dream House* features the suave Cary Grant and the gorgeous Myrna Loy. *Freddie Steps Out* was a lesser-known movie of the day starring Freddie Stewart. The Fox continues to draw visitors from throughout the state and beyond with its eclectic mix of entertainment. (Then, courtesy Michael J. Semas; now, courtesy the author.)

Built at a cost of $217, 948.91 on the old Hanford Grammar School location, the Hanford Civic Auditorium was dedicated on May 22, 1925. A holdover from the school structure is the clock located in the building's facade, which keeps time for visitors taking advantage of the green grass, shady trees, and ice cream cones from the busy Superior Dairy located across Douty Street. (Both, courtesy the author.)

These two images show the fountain, "dedicated to the Pioneers of Kings County on May 6th, 1938," located in front of the Hanford Civic Auditorium. The grounds are surrounded by many historical structures, as well as businesses still in operation today. Community pride is centered in this significant Hanford location. The smaller drinking fountains that circled the large cascade were removed due to ongoing vandalism. Superior Dairy provides a backdrop for the modern image. (Both, courtesy the author.)

These two views of the Kings County Courthouse on Eighth Street between Irwin and Douty Streets show just how much foliage can grow in 110-plus years. Constructed in 1897 at a cost of $26,364, the structure was used by the county until 1977, when the county moved into a new state-of-the-art facility on West Lacey Boulevard. In 1914, the courthouse underwent a structural expansion towards the north. The job was done so well that it looks like it was originally designed that way. The structure went through additional remodelings in the 1980s, but not without numerous rumblings from local citizens, both for and against. Today, the building stands proudly and is considered one of the best in the city. Numerous tenants, including the Hanford Visitor Agency, operate within its walls. (Then, courtesy John Walker; now, courtesy the author.)

The small palm trees shown in this early image of the back of the old Hanford Grammar School are still growing strong some 86 years later. Today's visitors now see them as an entrance to the Veteran's Memorial Hall and Civic Park. The hall was constructed in 1925 and is home to American Legion Post No. 3. Built at a cost of $46,000, the structure doubles as a senior center today. The grammar school building was demolished, and the beautiful Civic Auditorium building now stands in its place. (Then, courtesy Michael J. Semas; now, courtesy the author.)

Construction on the Kings County Jail began in 1897 and was completed on November 1, 1898. The county used the facilities up until 1964, when a new facility was built. A part of Hanford lore is that the building is haunted. The castle-type turret still looks as ominous as ever in the 21st century. (Both, courtesy the author.)

These two views of the Superior Dairy Products Company show that the structure has not changed much has changed since it first opened on February 8, 1930. F.J. Bowden, a manager at the Lucerne Creamery, broke ground on his vision in the fall of 1929. Superior Dairy remains one the very best options the city has to offer for family fun. In 1935, the company's menu proudly proclaimed, "We manufacture only one grade of ice cream—the best." Thousands of annual visitors can attest that Bowden's winning philosophy has not changed a bit with time. (Then, courtesy the *Hanford Sentinel*; now, courtesy the author.)

Built in 1905 and 1906, the Carnegie library was gifted to the city by Andrew Carnegie. It served the community up until 1968, when a new library opened for business. Constructed at a cost of $12,500, the building is now home to the Hanford Carnegie Museum. The vintage image shows the structure as it looked in 1920. (Both, courtesy the author.)

This Frank and Lena Bettencourt residence, located on Irwin Street just south of Grangeville, was built in 1929. Originally in the country, the home is surrounded today by shopping facilities, schools, and hundreds of residences. The house stands as an example of the many beautiful historic homes dotting the community's landscape north of downtown Hanford. (Both, courtesy the author.)

This home, located at 119 West Ivy Street, still stands today. Businessman Tom Esrey owned the house while he operated the Esrey Hotel in the Opera House Building, at Seventh and Irwin Streets. Esrey also dabbled in a wholesale liquor business, which apparently was as well known as his hospitality enterprise. (Then, courtesy Michael J. Semas; now, courtesy the author.)

Located near the northwest corner of Grangeville Boulevard and Douty Street, the new Hanford High School campus opened on September 26, 1921, at a cost of nearly $500,000. The building was a source of community pride all the way up to its demolition in 1975. The structure had suffered damage from a 1952 earthquake and, in later years, was deemed unsafe and did not meet new California earthquake standards. To this day, the citizens of Hanford continue to voice their frustration that the building was not retrofitted and that it was replaced with a structure that some compare to a prison. (Both, courtesy the author.)

Looking east on Seventh Street between Green and White Streets, this view show the early Chinese shops that lined the north side of the road in 1933. Today, construction is ongoing. The large foreground building is currently being remodeled as a teahouse to be operated by Steve Banister and Arianne Wing, two champions for improvement of the China Alley Historic District. (Then, courtesy Michael J. Semas; now, courtesy the author.)

The earlier image shows off the beautiful China Cafe neon sign as it appeared in the early 1980s. Today, the structure is unoccupied. The modern photograph shows the L.T. Sue Herb Building, located next door in the China Alley Historic District. The Herb Building is scheduled for major restoration work, as it has suffered the sands of time more than any of the other beautiful buildings in the district. Many photographers have earned their stars taking photographs of this historic structure. (Both, courtesy the author.)

The Hanford Post Office, shown here under construction in 1914, opened January 1, 1916. The building is located on the southwest corner of Eighth and Douty Streets. The location served the postal needs of the community into the early 1960s and then was home to the Kings County Justice Court until 1977. Today, the building remains one of Hanford's prettiest structures and serves as home to a Rabobank branch. (Both, courtesy the author.)

The Hanford Pool, also known as the Plunge, opened in 1938 at a cost of $30,000. The building and pool were demolished in the late 1980s and replaced with a modern swimming facility. Today, the pool serves the young and old as relief from the hot Central Valley summers and also provides a training facility for members of the Hanford and Kings County Fire Departments. (Both, courtesy the author.)

These views show the Hanford Fire Department station on Lacey Boulevard, west of Kaweah Street. Construction on the building was completed in 1939, and it replaced the structure that had stood on Douty Street since 1894. (Both, courtesy the author.)

With the involvement of the United States in World War II in the 1940s, the government began asking cities to start collecting scrap metal for various uses in the war. It was decided that the 640-pound bell at the old Douty Street Fire Department would be taken down and donated to the war effort. Local citizens banded together and hid the bell in a pile of grain at Lacey Milling Company. After being proudly displayed at the Lacey Boulevard firehouse for a number of years, the bell was relocated to the newer Grangeville Boulevard Station when it was constructed in 1988. The modern image shows fireman Scott Melon standing beside one of Hanford's treasures. (Then, courtesy the Kings County Library; now, courtesy the author.)

Sitting proudly on the left in what is believed to be the first sheriff's car in the state of California is former sheriff William Van Buckner. Beside Buckner sits Harry Bernstein. Standing nearby is then sheriff William Kimes. The old county jail is behind the three gentlemen, and a busy Douty Street can be seen in the background in this 1927 image. Today's law enforcement vehicles, such as the Hanford Police Department patrol car in the modern photograph, are loaded with various electronic equipment including computers, scanners, and speed detectors—items that Sheriff Buckner could never have dreamed of. (Then, courtesy John Walker; now, courtesy the author.)